Arise my son, follow here in the wake of my voice to the place frequented of all.

PINDAR

But apparently children also needed the random stranger who crossed their path: on crowded boulevards, in supermarkets and subway stations, time and time again the adult found his only certainty in those wide-open, almost unblinking eyes at a level with a grownup's waist, which took in every individual in the largest crowd, on the lookout for a responsive glance. The passerby could count on their helpful notice.

Then he realized that the modern times he had so often cursed and rejected did not exist, and that the "end of time" was also a figment of the brain. The same possibilities were reborn with every new consciousness, and the eyes of children in a crowd —just look at them!—transmitted the eternal spirit. Woe unto you who fail to see those eyes.

PETER HANDKE

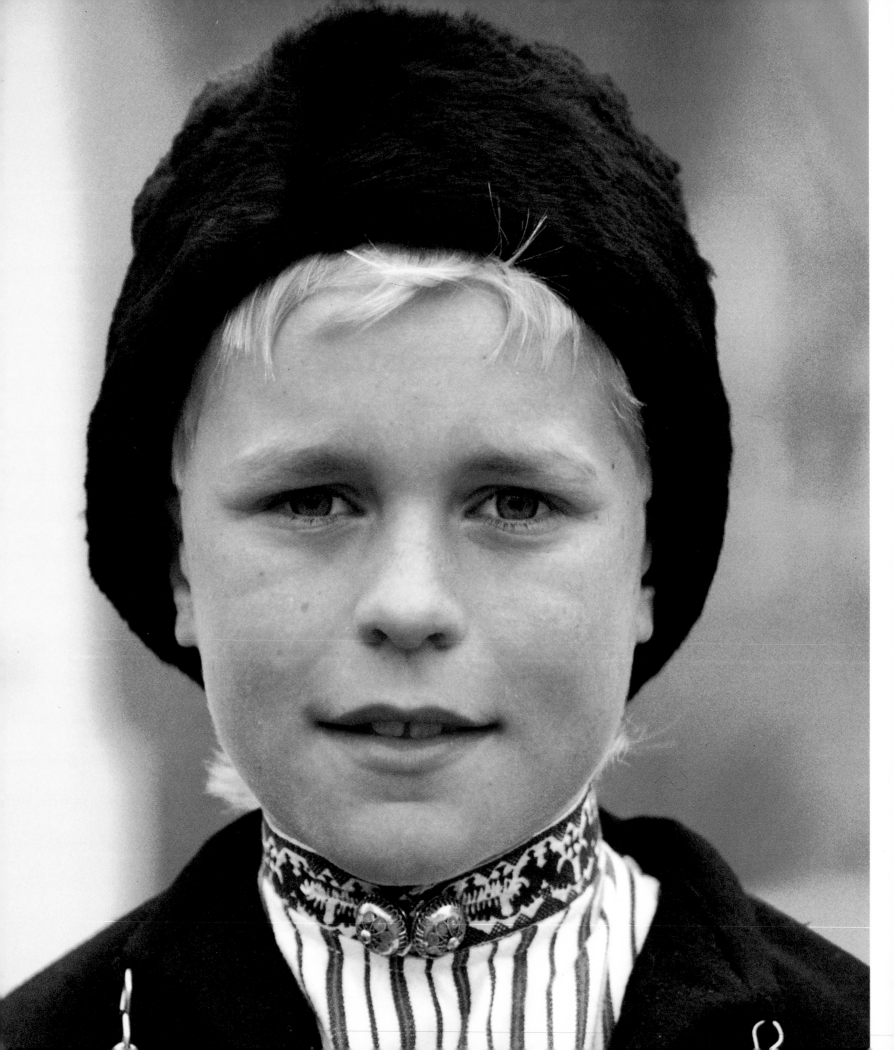

Papa, don't scold!

Mama, don't nag!

Come aside

And see my skill

In making myself

A beauty here.

My hair jade black,

My makeup a blend

Of lovely rouge

To put on my face.

Reddened lips

And blackened brows.

My hair is full

Of pearls and silver

And purest gold.

Jewels and trinkets on me,

Hanging, tinkling together!

Will you give them to me?

How can you abandon me?

CHINESE TALE

"Child, you look so astonishing,

where are you coming from today?"

"I'm looking for my mother."

"I am your mother!"

"Where did you give birth to me?"

"I gave birth to you under a dooki."

"What did you cover me with?"

"I covered you with dooki leaves."

"Then you are my mother!"

All at once, the mother threw down her pestle.

She dashed into the house.

The ostrich followed her.

The mother found the father.

And told him: "I've found my child!"

They cried out.

The father seized a bull and threw it to the ground.

He performed the ceremony of name giving.

He gave the child a name.

This tale jumps from here,

It stops over there.

ALDIOUMA DIALLO

15

My friends are strange:
A Jew, a Berber, a Hottentot,
An Arab, an Indian, a Zulu,
A meztiso from I don't know who
And I don't know where.

I don't know how
But they manage to communicate
With serious words
Bursting into vain laughter.
My friends are strange,
Don't you think?

MALICK FALL

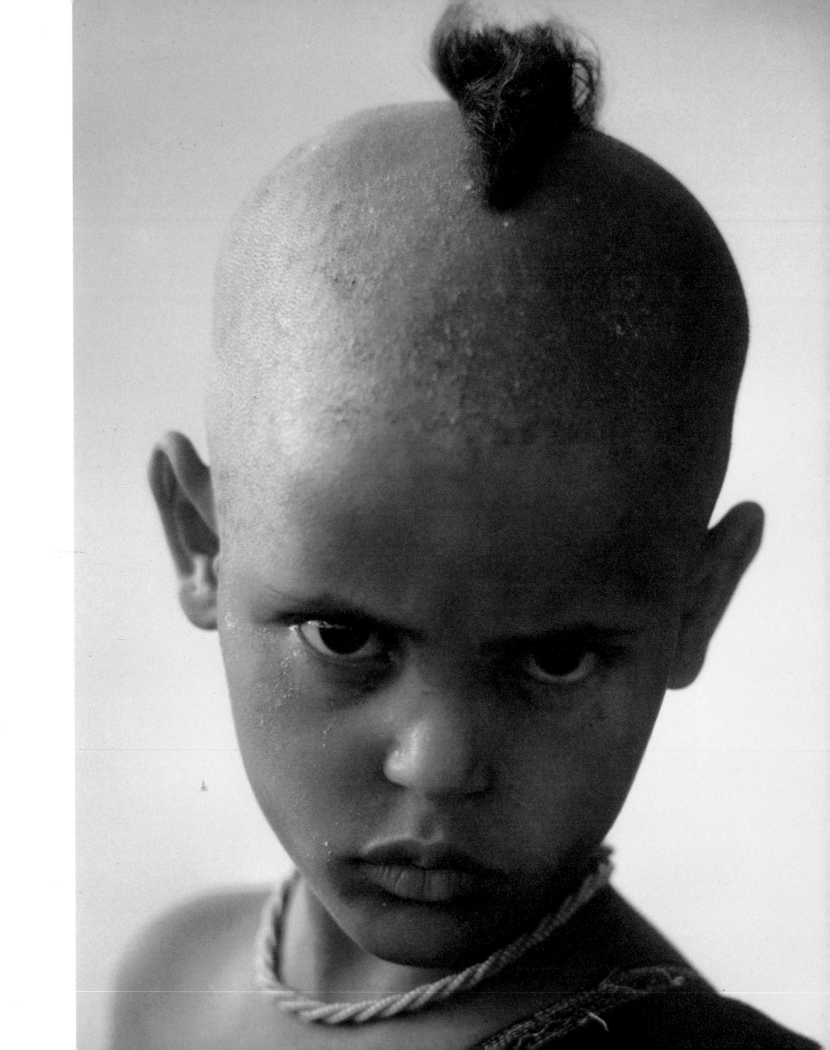

We
the Children

W.W. NORTON & COMPANY
NEW YORK • LONDON

UNICEF ADVISERS
Claire Brisset
Tony Carvalho
Janet Nelson
Ann Winter

ARTISTIC DIRECTION
Jean-Claude Suares

PHOTOGRAPHIC RESEARCH
Laura Resen, New York.
Tsuguo Tada, Tokyo.

PHOTOGRAPHIC SELECTION
Jim Mairs, New York.
Patrick Dufour, Paris.

LITERARY RESEARCH
Eve J. Picower, New York.
Menehould de Bazelaire, Paris,
Fabienne Rostand, Paris.

COMPOSITION
Frédéric Katz, Paris.

COLOR SEPARATIONS
Pioneer Graphic Scanning, Petaling Jaya, Malaysia.

PRINTING AND BINDING
Mohndruck, Gütersloh, Germany.

PHOTOGRAPHS
Abbas *Magnum* 100-101, 159, 166
P. Artinian *Vu* 131
D. Austen *After Image* 51
B. Barbey *Magnum* 110-111, 153, 170, 196-197
P. Bartolomew *Gamma* 14
E. Bazan 86-87, 104-105, 163
C. Bernson *Black Star* 189
M. Biber *Gamma* 85
G. Biddle 150
R. Bishop *After Image* 82
C. Boisvieux 5, 43, 94, 154, 171, 204, 207, 218
E. Brissaud *Gamma* 97
J. Bryson *Image Bank* 65
G. Champlong *Image Bank* 3
A. Chenevière 1, 7, 37, 52-53, 138-138, 200
L. Choquer *Métis* 2
J. Cooke 39, 41, 54, 151 (bottom)
B. Davidson *Magnum* 219
B. Descamps *Vu* 79 (top)
S. Doherty *Gamma* 155
V. Englebert *Photo Researchers* 141
M. Epstein 201
J. Fields *After Image* 11, 38, 176-177
S. Franklin *Magnum*

180-181, 216
R. Frerck *After Image* 209
Gabriel *Vu* 33, 35
B. Gibson *Visions* 48
J. Gordon 210-211
H. Gruyaert *Magnum* 88-89
E. Hoffman *Archives pictures* 17, 161
C. Harbutt *Actuality* 45
D. Hurn *Magnum* 83
G. Iturbide *Vu* 95
J. Isaac 145
R. Jope *Photo Researchers* 185
R. Kalvar *Magnum* 78 (bottom)
H. Kubota *Magnum* 60-61, 99, 108-109, 178
H. Larson 102-103
D. Lefevre *Vu* 119
S. MacCurry *Magnum* 4, 9, 18, 21, 22, 45, 56-57, 59, 72, 169, 172, 174, 186, 190-191
M. E. Mark 45, 58, 107, 140, 142-143, 189, 213, 214-215
P. Marlow *Magnum* 122, 199
J. Nachtwey *Magnum* 115, 124-125, 126-127, 128-129, 130
G. Nilsen *Photo*

Researchers 55
K. Nomachi 148-149, 173, 187, 202, 205
Obremski *Image Bank* 8
P. Parrot *Sygma* 144
J. Passow *J.B. Picture* 121
G. Peress *Magnum* 49, 66, 160
C. S. Perkins *Magnum* 106
Raghu-Rai *Magnum* 73
E. Reed *Magnum* 217
G. Rossi *Image Bank* 19
G. Rowell 193
M. Salas *Image Bank* 13, 137
S. Salgado *Magnum* 46-47, 116-117
F. Scianna *Magnum* 93, 96, 175
T. Scennet *Magnum* 151 (top)
J. M. Simon *Vision* 118
N. Slavin 70-71
W. Stone *Bruce Coleman* 12, 161, 194-195
A. Tannenbaum *Sygma* 42
T. Tanuma 67, 68, 78 (top), 107 (top), 147, 164, 188 (bottom), 203
P. Taylor *Bruce*

Coleman 161
P. Turnley *Black Star* 16
M. Vimenet *Vu* 79 (bottom)
A. Webb *Magnum* 75
S. Winter 45, 150 (bottom), 188
J. Wolf *Gamma* 167
J. T. Wright *Bruce Coleman* 161
M. Wright *Blackimages* 74

Tonga   Pakistan   USSR   Kenya   Nepal

Ireland   Ecuador   Netherlands   India   Panama

Papua   China   India   Israel   Laos

Iraq   Kenya   Mali   Afghanistan

Crimes Against Childhood

ELIE WIESEL

Somewhere in Asia, in a refugee camp near the Cambodian border. A little boy with an emaciated body stares at me. His huge eyes reflect an old man's hopelessness. Why is he gazing at me? I have no idea. Does he want me to give him something? I offer him a few dollars; he does not take them. I hold out a bar of chocolate. My offering is rejected. The rejection startles me. All at once, I am filled with shame. This child wants something from me, or from the world, and I have no right not to know what it is. I ask him in English, in French, in all the languages that I know, whether he is hungry, thirsty, whether he has parents, what his name is; he does not understand. All he does is to keep staring at me with strange, baffling eyes.

Was he intent on telling me that he expected nothing from me, from us? That it was too late to make good the injustice committed against him? Too late to save him? Today, I am still haunted by his eyes, which were filled with nameless sorrow and endless wisdom.

We must love God, the Scriptures tell us. And love others, our fellow man. And the stranger. But the children? There is no divine commandment telling us to love them. For such love is instinctive. It is part of our being, it illustrates the humanity of our being. We do not need to be reminded of it. Is it necessary to tell us that we have to breathe in order to stay alive? Human beings are made in such a way that, for obvious reasons, we love our children more than ourselves.

The children are both our near and distant future. It is by them and through them that we feel linked to the immortality of the human race. Children give their parents a sense of power and vulnerability in absolute terms: thanks to the children, infinity has a human face, which pain can disfigure, which death can reduce to dust and ashes.

That is why we invest so much of ourselves in the children. Children must live so that we ourselves can survive. Our children must grow and blossom so that our lives do not end in defeat. Are these dreams too heavy for the frail shoulders of the children? It's for their own good too, we tell ourselves. It's for their common future. Are not the children, by definition, the bearers of promise?

For ourselves, the children also have pasts, our past. Gazing at children, it is them themselves that we see again. The children remind us of our own childhood, when anything seemed possible. For this reason, we can only love the children all the more.

And yet, society is often the enemy of the children. In Antiquity, we hurled them from mountain tops or immolated them on altars. Later on, we consecrated them to the gods or sold them into slavery before sacrificing them in the name of all imaginable causes and ideals. To save themselves, people killed the children. Could they have been subconsciously jealous of their offspring, who would survive them? This claim is made by certain researchers. A hypothesis that would explain an individual's mindset. But how are we to understand the mindset of a group, a community, or a group of communities?

It is as if society tried to abuse the innocence of the children in order to plunge them into a universe of criminal violence. How many children have recently perished in wars and conflicts virtually throughout the globe? The adults fought one another, and it was the children who were killed. It is as if the world wanted to profit from their powerlessness in order to humiliate them by reducing them to starvation, to the miseries of exile, to all forms of agony and despair.

Naturally, I do not mean the privileged children who live in the rich, industrialized countries. I am speaking mainly about the children of so-called underdeveloped nations. I am speaking about the children I met in Asian refugee camps. And the ones I discovered in Latin America. A recent statistic demonstrates the tragedy of children: their mortality rate is terrifying—a child dies every minute. In other words: while my hand wrote this text, eighty to a hundred children died of exhaustion, hunger, or illnesses caused by famine.

Are we guilty of heartlessness? Lack of compassion? Let us call it a lack of imagination. We, today, love our children; but we are more or less indifferent to other people's children, especially if they are far away. Since we cannot see them, we fail to imagine them as they are somewhere else, on the other side, always on the other side: weak and frail, capable of tenderness and vulnerable to pain, ready to receive anything: to discover anything, to return fivefold anything that is given to them.

If we are incapable of seeing all children as our own, we will never have anything more than hope.

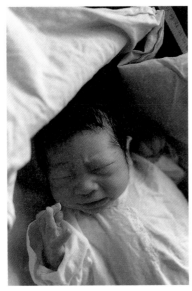

We, the Children

Birth and First
Steps

The Learning
Process

Ceremonies

Dangers and Fears   Friendship   Rites of Passage   Work and Play

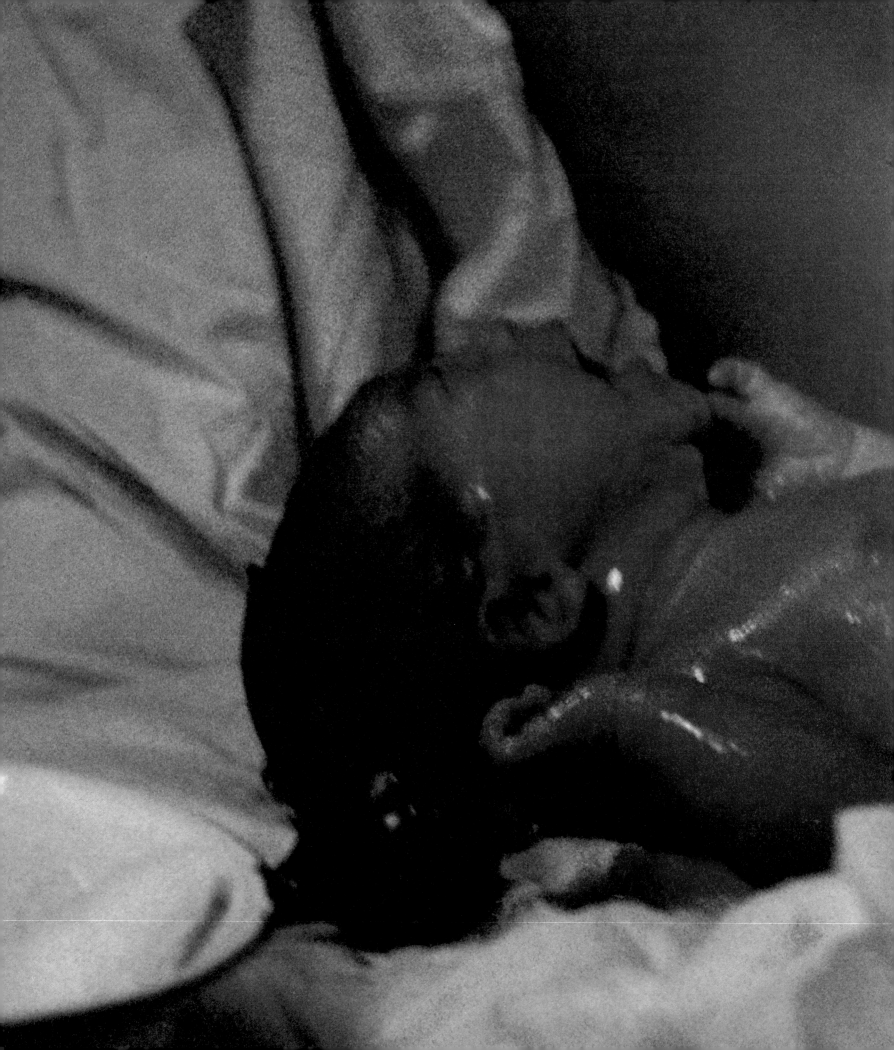

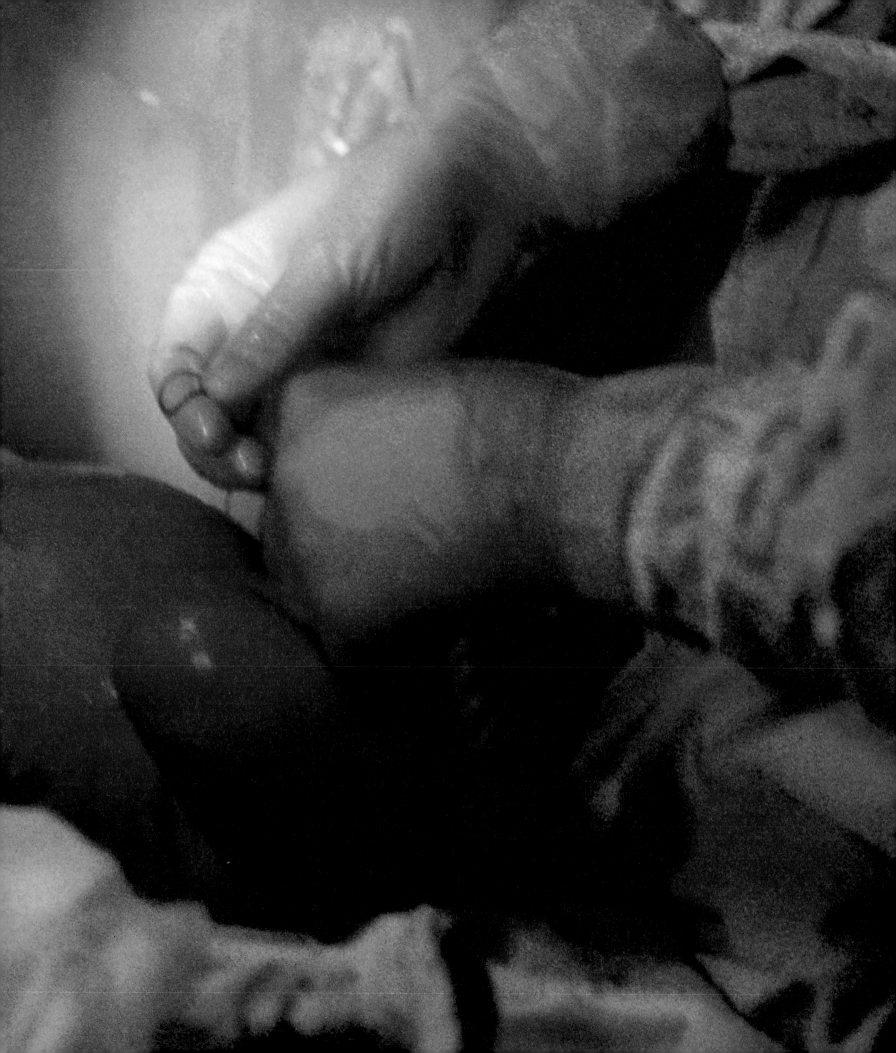

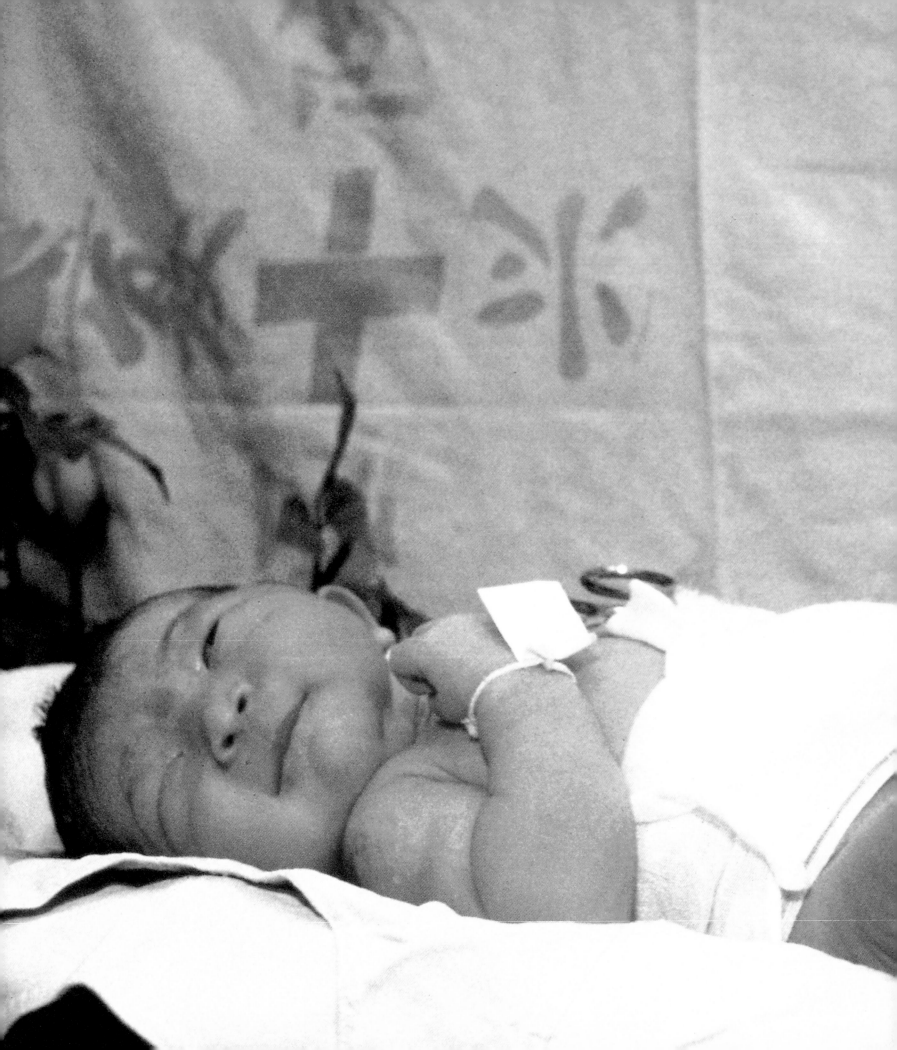

小

宝宝的芳名 _____

出生时间 ___ 年 ___ 日

属相 _____ 体重 ___ 克

母亲 _____ 时年 ___ 岁

家庭成员

_____

_____

生于

医院、接生医师

Give to these children, new from the world,
Silence and love;
And the long dew-dropping hours of the night,
And the stars above:

Give to these children, new from the world,
Rest far from men.
Is anything better, anything better?
Tell us it then:

Us who are old, old and gay,
O so old!
Thousands of years, thousands of years,
If all were told.

WILLIAM BUTLER YEATS

PAGES 32-33 AND 34-35
China - Beijing - newborn at a maternity hospital

Ecuador - near Santo Domingo - Colorados tribe newborn

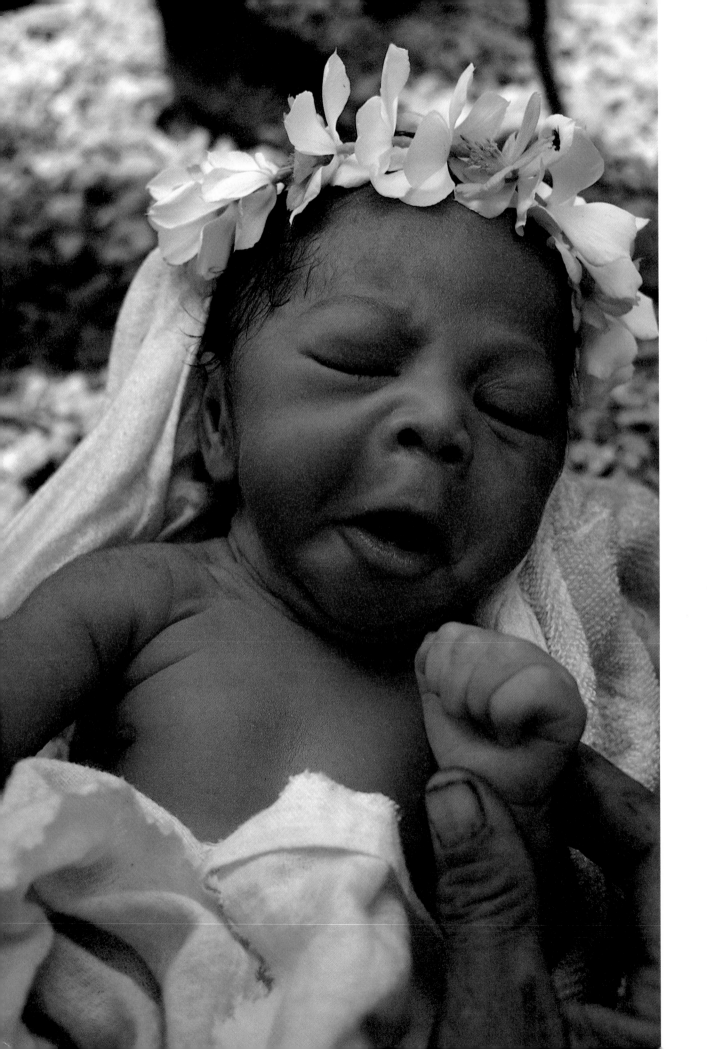

Micronesie - Ifalitk
baptism of a child

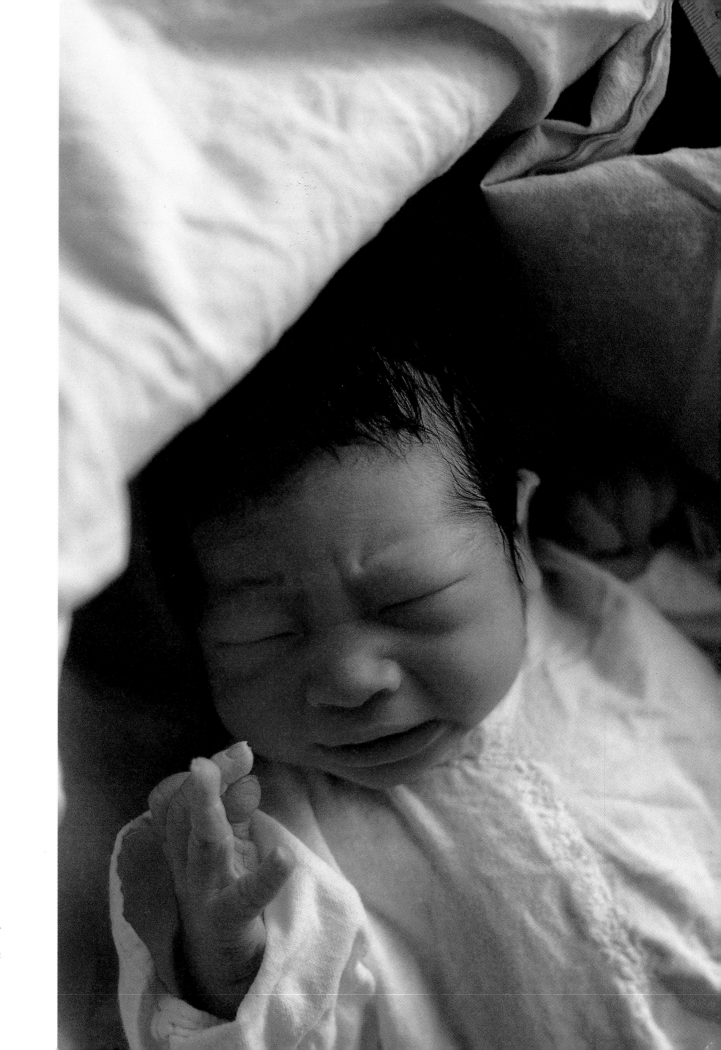

China - Shanghai
newborn

"I have no name,
I am but two days old."
What shall I call thee?
"I happy am,
Joy is my name."
Sweet joy befall thee!

Pretty joy!
Sweet joy but two days old,
Sweet joy I call thee;
Thou dost smile,
I sing the while—
Sweet joy befall thee.

WILLIAM BLAKE

USSR - Moscow - baptism in the Church of the Old Believers

And a woman who held a babe against her bosom said, Speak to us of Children. And he said: Your children are not your children. They are the sons and daughters of Life's longing for itself. They come through but not from you, and though they are with you, yet they belong not to you. You may give them your love but not your thoughts. For they have their own thoughts. You may house their bodies but not their souls, for their souls dwell in the house of tomorrow, which you cannot visit, not even in your dreams. You may strive to be like them, but seek not to make them like you. For life goes not backward nor tarries with yesterday. You are the bows from which your children as living arrows are sent forth. The archer sees the mark upon the path of the infinite, and He bends you with His might that His arrows may go swift and far. Let your bending in the archer's hand be for gladness; for even as he loves the arrow that flies, so He loves also the bow that is stable.

KAHLIL GIBRAN

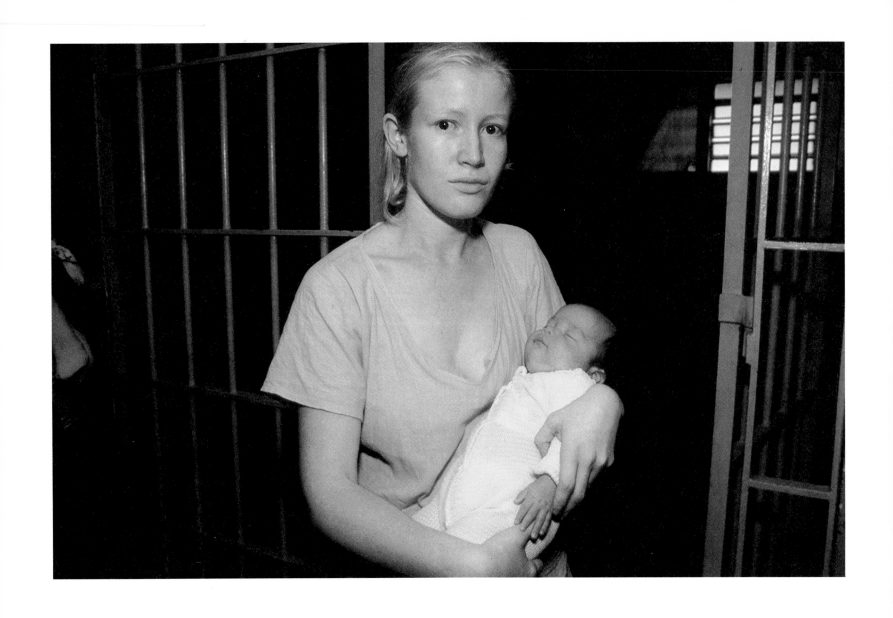

"Where have I come from, where did you pick me up?" the baby asked its mother. She answered, half crying, half laughing, and clasping the baby to her breast, "You were hidden in my heart as its desire, my darling. (...) You were enshrined with our household deity, in his worship I worshipped you.

In all my hopes and my loves, in my life, in the life of my mother you have lived.

In the lap of the deathless Spirit who rules our home you have been nursed for ages. (...) Heaven's first darling, twin-born with the morning light, you have floated down the stream of the world's life, and at last you have stranded on my heart. As I gaze on your face, mystery overwhelms me; you who belong to all have become mine. For fear of losing you I hold you tight to my breast. What magic has snared the world's treasure in these slender arms of mine?"

RABINDRANATH TAGORE

OPPOSITE PAGE

Papua New Guinea - albino child

PAGES 52-53

Bolivia - Tarabuquenos tribe - mother and daughter

USSR - Moscow - grandmother and grandchild

LEFT
India - New Dehli
old man and child
with cobras

RIGHT
France - Marseille
Spanish gypsies

PAGES 60-61
China - Sinkiang
near Urumchi
a Kazakh family
in the Tianshan
Ranges

The School Teacher of Carrasqueda

MIGUEL DE UNAMUNO

Always let the heart speak, children: it sees clearly, even if it does not see far away. You are summoned to a town to settle a quarrel that may cause a lot of bloodshed. On the way, you hear the anguished cries of a child who has fallen into a well. Are you going to let him drown? Are you going to say: "I can't stop, my child, a whole town is waiting for me to save it." Not at all! Obey your heart! Stop, dismount, and save the child! Let the town wait! Some day, this child may become the guide or savior, not only of a single town, but of many cities.

That was what Don Casiano, the school teacher of Carrasqueda, always told several of the older pupils, who, as he spoke, gazed at him with eyes that seemed to be listening. But did they understand him? That was a question that Don Casiano, in his capacity as a decent teacher, never asked himself when he poured his heart out to his class. "They may not understand every last syllable," he would tell himself, "but as for the music. . . ."

God has not blessed his marriage with children, but Don Casiano thought of Ramonet as his own son, and through him, the village, indeed all of Carrasqueda, as his children. "I will make a man of you," the teacher told him, "I will make a man of you. Let yourself be loved."

And Ramonet yielded and let himself be loved. The teacher imbued him with his own ambitions and the lofty aspirations that, without his knowing how, had drowsed off in his heart. In the sown fields, under the infinite vault of the sky, the teacher, surrounded by his pupils, and with Ramonet at his side, poured out his heart to them. . . .

When those children had become men, with families of their own, they would gather at his home every Sunday for a reading that he would comment on. He cleansed their bodies and minds, taught them how to recover and utilize the fertilizers, and, above all, preserve the innocence of perpetual childhood deep in their hearts.

Children when they come first into it, are surrounded with a world of new things, which, by a constant solicitation of their senses, draw the mind constantly to them; forward to take notice of the new, and apt to be delighted with the variety of changing objects. Thus the first years are usually employed and diverted in looking abroad.

JOHN LOCKE

The greatness of the human personality begins at the hour of birth. From this almost mystic affirmation there comes what may seem a strange conclusion: that education must start from birth.

MARIA MONTESSORI

OPPOSITE PAGE
Qatar - girl's primary school

PAGES 70-71
South Africa - near Port Elizabeth - "little flower school"

Japan - Osaka - Korean school

Tibet - Dharamsala - Tibetan refugees learning to brush their teeth at school

Nepal - novice monks

ABOVE

Haiti - Bombardopolis - school prayer

PAGES 76-77

Korea - Seoul - young girls before sports event

75

ABOVE
*Japan - Tokyo
contest of personal
computer game in
Shinjuku*

RIGHT
*Japan - Tokyo
kindergarten class*

China - Kweilin - kindergarten students

Great Britain - Wales - Claerleon - dance rehearsal

A man is born gentle and weak.

At his death he is hard and stiff.

Green plants are tender and filled with sap.

At their death they are withered and dry.

Therefore the stiff and unbending

is the disciple of death.

The gentle and yielding is the disciple of life.

Thus an army without flexibility

never wins a battle.

A tree that is unbending is easily broken.

The hard and the strong will fall.

The soft and the weak will overcome.

LAO-TSU

ABOVE
Albania - Tirana - ballet class

PAGES 86-87
Thailand - Site 2 - Cambodian children

PAGES 88-89
Belgium - Louviere - Mardi-Gras

85

Childhood, Boyhood and Youth

LEO TOLSTOY

O happy, happy time of childhood, never to be recalled! How could one fail to love and cherish one's memories of it? These memories refresh and elevate my soul and are for me the source of all my best pleasures. (...)

And then, afterward, when you were already upstairs and kneeling before the icons in your little quilted dressing gown, what a wonderful feeling it would be to say: "God bless Daddy and God bless Mummy." Repeating those prayers, which my childish lips had first lisped after my mother, my love for her and my love for God somehow strangely merged into a single feeling.

After prayers you would roll yourself in your little quilt; your heart would feel light and bright and joyful; dreams put other dreams to flight—but what were they? They were fleeting, but filled with pure love and hopes for radiant happiness. (...) Again you'd pray for God to make everyone happy, for everyone to be content and for there to be nice weather for going out the next day; then you'd turn on your other side, your thoughts and dreams would get all tangled up and confused and you'd drop quietly, peacefully off to sleep, your face still wet with tears.

Will they ever return, that freshness, that innocence, that need for love and strength of faith that one possessed in childhood? What time could ever be better than the time when the two greatest virtues—innocent gaiety and a boundless appetite for love—were one's sole incentives in life?

Where are those ardent prayers? Where the supreme gift—those tears of tender emotion? One's guardian angel would fly down, wipe away those tears with a smile and waft sweet dreams into that unspoiled, childish imagination.

Unlike ours, the child's creative faith is still unbro-ken, and he does not yet carry the seed of destructive reason. He is innocent and therefore wise. He understands better than we the ineffable key to poetic substance.

FEDERICO GARCIA LORCA

Italy - Sicily - young girls dressed as Saints during ceremony in Marsala

Ireland - Croagh Patrick pilgrimage

Mexico - Chalma - religious procession

Italy - Sicily - Enna - Good Friday parade

USSR - Estonia - Talin - traditionnal annual festival

And God has made for you

Mates (and Companions) of your own nature,

And made for you, out of them,

Sons and daughters and grandchildren

And provided for you sustenance

Of the best

Wealth and sons are allurements

Of the life of this world

THE KORAN

OPPOSITE PAGE

China - Sinkiang - Kashgar - at Id Kah Mosque

PAGES 100-101

*Malaysia - the "Arquam" (fundamentalist Muslim sect) community of Teluk Intan,
girls memorizing The Koran*

PAGES 102-103

Pakistan - Kashmir - Azad

PAGES 104-105

Thailand - novice monks

ABOVE : *Kenya - Nairobi wedding ceremony*

OPPOSITE PAGE :
Northern Ireland - Belfast first communion

LEFT : *Zimbabwe - Harare*

PAGES 108-109
Burma - Inle Lake initiation ceremony

PAGES 110-111
France - Corsica - children of Foreign Legion soldiers

The Children of the Future

JULIEN GREEN

An unhappy childhood is an indictment of all humanity. Whatever his skin color—black, yellow, or white—a child that is starved, for food or affection, puts us to shame. More than at any time, perhaps, this small, gaunt face gazes at us with unendurable eyes—unendurable, because they pray for two simple things: bread and love. Give the child both, and his eyes will light up with joy. Christ loved children, he took them in his arms and hugged them. Children had their part in the miracle of the loaves and fishes. We have to learn how to put an end to this scandalous situation of their being human on the periphery of their great earthly adventure, without the joie de vivre for which they were meant and for which they will find no equivalent. We shudder at the thought of children being put into any kind of bondage, we shudder when reading stories that seem to come straight out of a bygone world, such as nineteenth-century England, which flew in the face of all ethics by forcing children to work. But Dickens took it upon himself to expose these horrors to the civilized world, and Victorian England took its little slaves out of its factories. Today —for instance, in Pakistan—children between the ages of six and ten are kidnapped and sold—sold for all conceivable purposes, including sexual ones. Yet Pakistan is being supplied with the means to produce nuclear weapons. These two situations are utterly incompatible with another! We barely have ten years left until the twenty-first century, which we hope will be different from all the previous centuries, with the weight of adult scorn for the young and the poor —who often are one and the same on this earth, which is so beautiful for them too. If the next ten years eliminate the hunger of children and make their beautiful, ignorant, and trusting eyes shine with the happiness of being understood and being among those to whom all our knowledge is offered, then we will have conquered a new world.

Hector - Don't you want to see him at all, not even for a moment? After that, you would think again. Do you mean never to see your son?

Andromache - It is your son that interests me. Hector, it's because he is yours, because he is you, that I'm so afraid. You don't know how like you he is. Even in this no-man's-land where he is waiting, he already has everything, all those qualities you brought to this life we live together. He has your tenderness, your silences. If you love war, he will love it. Do you love war?

Hector - Why ask such a question?

Andromache - Admit, sometimes you love it.

Hector - If a man can love what takes away hope, and happiness, and all those nearest to his heart.

JEAN GIRAUDOUX

OPPOSITE PAGE
Guatemala - Guatemala City - Armed Forces Day parade

PAGES 116-117
Mali - Sahel - victims of famine

Guatemala - Adolfo Hall Military School - twelve year old cadets training

Afghanistan - Ghazni

—A simple Child,

That lightly draws its breath,

And feels its life in every limb,

What should it know of death?

I met a little cottage Girl:

She was eight years old, she said;

Her hair was thick with many a curl

That clustered round her head. (...)

"Sisters and brothers, little Maid,

How many may you be?"

"How many? Seven in all," she said,

And wondering looked at me. (...)

Then did the little Maid reply,

"Seven boys and girls are we;

Two of us in the church-yard lie,

Beneath the church-yard tree." (...)

"But they are dead, those two are dead!

There spirits are in heaven!"

"Twas throwing words away; for still

The little Maid would have her will,

And said, "Nay, we are seven!"

WILLIAM WORDSWORTH

Israel - Beit Safara - Palestinian boy wearing a red and white kafiya, with friends

ABOVE
Northern Ireland - Belfast

PAGES 124-125
*Guatemala - Quiche Dpt - Finca La Perla - children and defense forced to guard
against guerillas*

PAGES 126-127
El Salvador

PAGES 128-129
El Salvador - Tecoluca - suspected rebel shot and buried by the army

Only the eyes are open

In this face torn by the mare of the plains

The body caught fire

When the child clung to the vine shoot

To keep from leaving the earth

Only his eyes were open

In the twilight of the sand

And the charred hand remained suspended

Stretching towards the entrance to the sky

As if to greet a friend

When the horseman repulsed

The storm with a gesture

Leaving the pages of the manuscript

For absence and death

In the desert of this people devoted to breaking. . .

TAHAR BEN JELLOUN

Lebanon - Litani River - victims of Israeli attack

Armenia - earthquake victim

The Little Prince

Antoine de Saint-Exupery

ne only understands the things that one tames, said the fox. Men have no more time to understand anything. They buy things already made at the shops. But there is no shop anywhere where one can buy friendship, and so men have no friends any more. If you want a friend, tame me. . .

- What must I do, to tame you? asked the little prince.

-You must be very patient, replied the fox. First you will sit down at a little distance from me—like that—in the grass. I shall look at you out of the corner of my eye, and you will say nothing. Words are the source of misunderstandings. But you will sit a little closer to me, every day. . . The next day the little prince came back.

- It would have been better to come back at the same hour, said the fox. If, for example, you come at four o'clock in the afternoon, then at three o'clock I shall begin to be happy. I shall feel happier and happier as the hour advances. At four o'clock, I shall already be worrying and jumping about. I shall show you how happy I am! But if you come at just any time, I shall never know at what hour my heart is to be ready to greet you. . . One must observe the proper rites. . .

- What is a rite? asked the little prince.

- Those also are actions too often neglected, said the fox. They are what make one day different from other days, one hour from other hours. There is a rite, for example, among my hunters. Every Thursday they dance with the village girls. So Thursday is a wonderful day for me! I can take a walk as far as the vineyards! But if the hunters danced at just any time, every day would be like every other day, and I should never have any vacation at all.

So the little prince tamed the fox. And when the hour of his departure drew near:

- Ah, said the fox, I shall cry.

- It is your own fault, said the little prince. I never wished you any sort of harm; but you wanted me to tame you. . .

- Yes, that is so, said the fox.

- But now you are going to cry! said the little prince.

- Yes, that is so, said the fox.

- Then it has done you no good at all!

- It has done me good, said the fox, because of the color of the wheat fields.

And then he added:

- Go and look again at the roses. You will understand now that yours is unique in all the world. Then come back to say goodbye to me, and I will make you a present of a secret.

The little prince went away, to look again at the roses.

- You are not at all like my rose, he said. As yet you are nothing. No one has tamed you, and you have tamed no one. You are like my fox when I first knew him. He was only a fox like a hundred thousand other foxes. But I have made him my friend, and now he is unique in all the world.

And the roses were very much embarrassed.

- You are beautiful, but you are empty, he went on. One could not die for you. To be sure, an ordinary passerby would think that my rose looked just like you—the rose that belongs to me. But in herself alone she is more important than all the hundreds of you other roses: because it is she that I have watered; because it is she that I have put under the glass globe; because it is she that I have sheltered behind the screen; because it is for her that I have killed the caterpillars (except the two or three that we saved to become butterflies); because it is she that I have listened to, when she grumbled, or boasted, or even sometimes when she said nothing. Because she is *my* rose.

And he went back to meet the fox.

- Goodbye, he said.

- Goodbye, said the fox. And now here is my secret, a very simple secret: It is only with the heart that one can see rightly; what is essential is invisible to the eye.

- What is essential is invisible to the eye, the little prince repeated, so that he would be sure to remember.

- It is the time you have wasted for your rose that makes your rose so important.

- It is the time I have wasted for my rose. . . said the little prince, so that he would be sure to remember.

- Men have forgotten this truth, said the fox. But you must not forget it. You become responsible, forever, for what you have tamed. You are responsible for your rose. . .

- I am responsible for my rose, the little prince repeated, so that

Polixenes -

We were, fair queen,

Two lads that thought there was no more behind

But such a day tomorrow as today,

And to be boy eternal.

Hermione -

Was not my lord

The verier wag o' th' two?

Polixenes -

We were as twinned lambs that did frisk i' th' sun,

And bleat the one at th' other; what we changed

Was innocence for innocence; we knew not

The doctrine of ill-doing, nor dreamed

That any did, had we pursued that life,

And our weak spirits ne'er been higher reared

With stronger blood, we should have answered heaven

Boldly, "not guilty"; the imposition cleared,

Hereditary ours.

WILLIAM SHAKESPEARE

OPPOSITE PAGE
China - Yuyang - schoolgirls in uniform

PAGES 138-139
Columbia - Guambianos tribe children

ABOVE
USA - children suffering from cancer

OPPOSITE PAGE
Brazil - Yanomami Indian boys in Amazon Jungle

PAGES 142-143
India - Bombay - young boys playing in the street

PAGE 144
France - Toulon

PAGE 145
India - Marayanpet

The wolf also shall dwell with the lamb, and the leopard shall lie down with the kid; and the calf and the young lion and the fatling together; and a little child shall lead them.

And the cow and the bear shall feed; their young ones shall lie together: and the lion shall eat straw like the ox.

And the sucking child shall play on the hole of the asp, and the weaned child shall put his hand on the cockatrice' den.

They shall not hurt nor destroy in all my holy mountain: for the earth shall be full of the knowledge of the Lord, as the waters cover the sea.

ISAIAH

OPPOSITE PAGE
Australia - Sydney - Koala Park

PAGES 148-149
Sudan - Nuel Tribe boys dancing while breeding cattle

ABOVE
USA - New York City
- young boxers

RIGHT
Haiti - children playing
in the street

ABOVE
*USA - North Dakota
Badlands - school in
Medora*

LEFT
*Canada - Winnipeg
hockey game*

"What a curious feeling!" said Alice. "I must be shutting up like a telescope!"

And so it was indeed: she was now only ten inches high, and her face brightened up at the thought that she was now the right size for going through the little door into that lovely garden. First, however, she waited for a few minutes to see if she was going to shrink any further: she felt a little nervous about this; "for it might end, you know," said Alice to herself, "in my going out altogether, like a candle. I wonder what I should be like then?" And she tried to fancy what the flame of a candle looks like after the candle is blown out, for she could not remember ever having seen such a thing.

LEWIS CARROLL

China - Shanghai - amusement park

ABOVE
Turkey - Göreme - schoolyard

OPPOSITE PAGE
Great Britain - Prebendal School students

The Moral Life of Children

ROBERT COLES

He lifted his face. He turned his body so that it received the wind directly. He closed his eyes. A big smile came over his face. When one gust hit him head on, he laughed. After a few minutes, as suddenly as it came, it went: no more wind; a silence noticeable by virtue of what had preceded it. A wait. Now the silence is the winner; it lasts and lasts. Eduardo's body begins to relax. He relents from his pose, turns around, lowers his head, takes a piece of chewing gum from his pocket, puts it in his mouth, begins to work on it. He offers a piece to me. I say no. He says that he should remember by now that I don't chew gum. Then this fragment out of a life's store of memories: "My mother used to give us gum when she had nothing else. Once I asked her what would happen if she had no gum. She told me not to ask her that, ever." An embarrassed further pause. The boy then observes my discomfort, decides to help out. He tells me again how much he likes the wind. I agree. Now we are once more in agreement, so to speak—with respect to gum, no, but with respect to wind, yes. Then this comment: "If had a choice, to pick the way I die, I'd choose to be carried off by the wind over to the ocean. I'd be made clean twice before I saw His face." The boy saw me turn quizzical at the use of a possessive pronoun. He had figured out my mind's question—a general skepticism finding its expression in a grammatical worry. What is the antecedent Eduardo had in mind? In a quiet voice, a whisper almost, he tells me: "God's face." He has learned after only ten years on earth to stay alive, to master a modern city, to spar with death, even anticipate its arrival, contemplate its many possibilities: a grown mind's moral imagination at work in the continuing life of one of this earth's vulnerable children.

The child contains the man he will become.

He is silent. But his face shows us (like a father)

The man who can still be barely sensed,

He carries him, guides him,

and conceals him inside himself.

Sometimes, as if to defend him—bravely.

If we look into the depth of children's eyes,

Into their gentle, innocent faces,

We would see him, linked, calm, and silent,

The man who will eventually explode (...)

Yes. In the park, we see the heedless child

Following a circle of moving colors;

Releasing innocent birds from its hands;

Tenderly stepping on the many bashful flowers,

But not squeezing out their vivid scents.

Happy, he shouts and runs towards us. In his smile

And in his joyous eyes, we, who are ignorant and airy,

Hasten to read the illusion of life

And his trusting appeal to our hearts.

VICENTE ALEIXANDRE

China - Xinjiang - Uygur boy

China - Beijing - municipal kindergarten

LEFT TO RIGHT

Japan

Thailand - Chiang Kham refugee camp - Yao Tribe

USSR - Ulyanovsk

Thailand

161

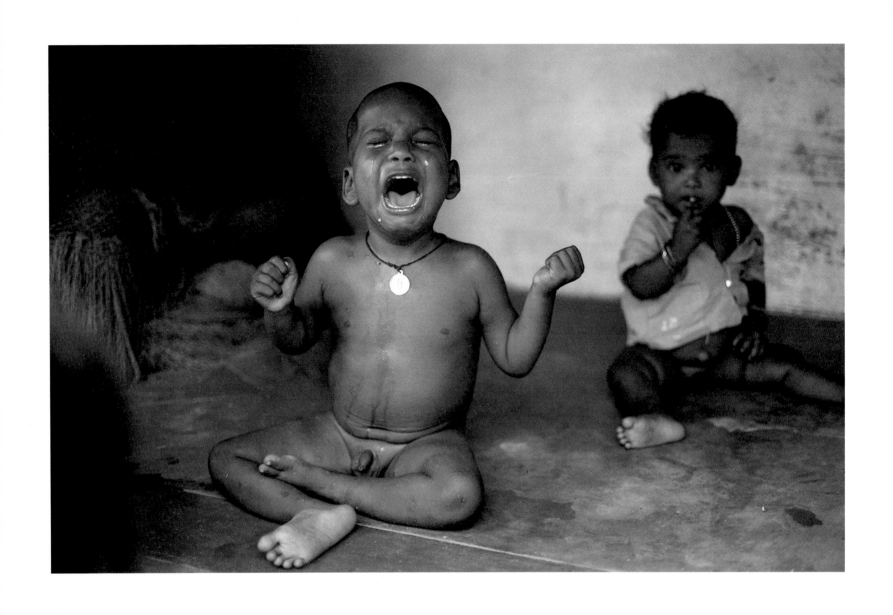

Columbia - Amazonia - Yagua child

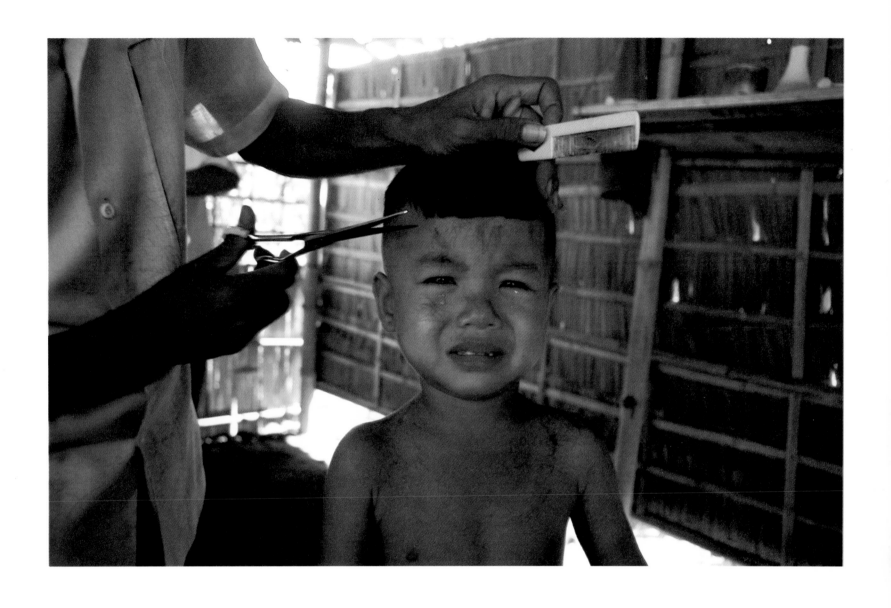

Thailand - Site 2 - Cambodian child in a refugee camp

PAGES 164-165
Czechoslovakia - Prague - public park

China - Muslim festival in Xian

USA- homeless child at a shelter

Why, the whole world of knowledge is not worth that child's prayer to 'dear, kind God'! (...) And if the suffering of children go to swell the sum of sufferings which was necessary to pay for truth, then I protest that the truth is not worth such a price. I don't want the mother to embrace the oppressor who threw her son to the dogs!

FYODOR DOSTOEVSKY

Bengladesh - near Dakha - young boy in the street

ABOVE

India - Rajasthan - Jaisalmer

OPPOSITE PAGE

Poland - Warsaw - Socialist May Day

Nepal
Kathmandu
young novice monk

Southern Soudan
Nuel tribe boy
ritual washing with
cow urine

ABOVE

France - Marseille - Spanish gypsies

OPPOSITE PAGE

Greece - Epirus - Lia village - a monk in a grocery store

PAGES 176-177

Ireland - young violonist

174

(...) All of childhood's unanswered questions must finally be passed back to the town and answered there. Heroes and bogey men, values and dislikes, are first encountered in that early environment. In later years they change faces, places and maybe races, tactics, intensities and goals, but beneath those penetrable masks they wear forever the stocking-capped faces of childhood.

MAYA ANGELOU

OPPOSITE PAGE
China - Shanghai - morning practice of Taiji

PAGES 180-181
Spain - Galicia - a family at home in the village of Sabugos

The Elfin King

GOETHE

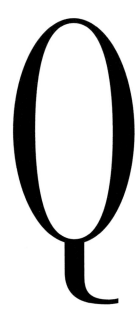Who rides by night in the wind so wild?
It is the father, with his child.
The boy is safe in his father's arm,
He holds him tight, he keeps him warm.

My son, what is it, why cover your face?
Father, you see him, there in that place,
The elfin king with his cloak and crown?
It is only the mist rising up, my son.

"Dear little child, will you come with me?
Beautiful games I'll play with thee;
Bright are the flowers we'll find on the shore,
My mother has golden robes fullscore."

Father, O father, and did you not hear
What the elfin king breathed into my ear?
Lie quiet, my child, now never you mind:
Dry leaves it was that click in the wind.

"Come along now, you're a fine little lad,

My daughters will serve you, see you are glad;

My daughters dance all night in a ring,

They'll cradle and dance you and lullaby sing."

Father, now look, in the gloom, do you see

The elfin daughters beckon to me?

My son, my son, I see it and say:

Those old willows, they look so gray.

"I love you, beguiled by your beauty I am,

If you are unwilling I'll force you to come!"

Father, his fingers grip me, O

The elfin king has hurt me so!

Now struck with horror the father rides fast,

His gasping child in his arm to the last,

Home through thick and thin he sped:

Locked in his arm, the child was dead.

One day, I was walking along a road, when I saw a child sitting at a crossroads. I asked him: "My child, which road goes to the city?"

He replied: "This one is long and short, and that one is short and long."

When I reached the city, it was surrounded by parks and gardens, and so I went back. I then asked the child: "My child, did you not tell me: 'This road is short'?"

He replied: "Rabbi, did I not say 'short and long'?"

I kissed him on the head, saying: "You are happy, children of Israel, for you are all wise, from your biggest to your smallest."

TALE FROM THE TALMUD

OPPOSITE PAGE

South of Ecuador - near Ingarpica - little Indian girl with her brothers

PAGE 186

India - Darjeeling - young Indian boy collecting firewood along train tracks

PAGE 187

China - Szechwan - girl milking a yak

ABOVE
*Honduras - children
swimming*

RIGHT
*France - Paris - children
playing soccer*

188

ABOVE
USA - New York - The Bronx - Richard Rogers Elementary School students

LEFT
Hong Kong - schoolboys sitting on a wall

PAGES 190-191
Mali - near Timbuktu boys fishing in the Niger river

Suffer little children, and forbid them not, to come unto me; for such is the kingdom of heaven. (...) Whosoever therefore shall humble himself as this little child, the same is greatest in the kingdom of heaven.

ST MATTHEW

There is always one moment in childhood when the door opens and lets the future in.

GRAHAM GREENE

USSR - amusement arcade

Guatemala - Quechua Indian

Egypt - Giza - Cheops Pyramid

China - Szechuan - Tibetan nomads moving

The United Arab Emirates - camel race

Ireland
Connemara

China - Kwangsi
female farmer
coming back
from field-work

Oman Sultanate - fisherboy on the Arabian coast with swordfish

Denmark - Féroé Island - Haldarsvick harbour - boy unloading fish

Behind the iron gate of an immense garden, at the back of which could be seen a charming chateau gleaming whitely in the sun, stood a beautiful, blooming little boy smartly dressed in country togs that are always so enchanting. (. . .) Beside him on the grass lay a magnificent toy, as blooming as its master. (. . .) But the child was paying no attention to his favorite toy, and this is what he was looking at: On the other side of the gate on the highway, standing in the midst of nettles and thistles, was another child, pitifully black and grimy, (. . .) Through the symbolic bars separating two worlds, highroad and mansion, the poor child was showing the rich child his own toy, which the latter was scrutinizing breathlessly, as though it had been some rare and unheard of object. Well, this toy that the grimy, little brat was shaking, teetering and turning in a box covered with wire, was a living rat! The parents out of economy, I suppose, had taken the toy from nature itself. And the two children were laughing together like brothers, with teeth of identical whiteness.

CHARLES BAUDELAIRE

ABOVE

Spain - Andalucia - Vejer de la Frontera - girls jumping rope

PAGES 210-211

Morocco - street scene

I was born a wild little girl of seven. Loosely clad in a slip of brown buckskin, and light-footed with a pair of soft moccasins on my feet, I was as free as the wind that blew my hair, and no less spirited than a bounding deer. (...) I was not wholly conscious of myself, but was more keenly alive to the fire within. It was as if I were the activity, and my hands and feet were only experiments for my spirit to work upon.

GERTRUDE SIMMONS BONNIN (ZITKALA-SA)

Hungary - hospital staff encouraging children suffering from spina bifida to walk

Malawi - Limbe - Monfort school for blind and deaf children

217

Canada - Vancouver - aquarium

USA - New York City - children on a subway